Join The Power to Rise Community on the CFC Rewards App

Claim and Redeem CFC Tokens for taking actionable steps!

Testimonials

"I had to take a moment to reflect on what was truly one of the most profound experiences of my life. When I was invited to a session with Christie, I didn't quite know what to expect. My only instruction before the call was to simply write down the name of a person or business—no other details or context. I got on the video call, and that's when the magic happened. The first name came up, and within seconds, Christie gave me an incredibly accurate and insightful assessment of the person or business I was referring to. Her ability to tap into such precise details without any prior information is nothing short of phenomenal.

If you're open to the possibilities that the Universe has to offer, you *must* experience this for yourself."

-Michael B.

Testimonials

"I have never experienced anyone like Christie Russ. I recall my first session being so uplifting --I could feel pure positive "let's get it done" physical energy through my entire body. She has helped me refine my vocabulary for my highest good and the good of humanity which in itself has been transformative. I also have a clear understanding and roadmap around my highest purpose, unique gifts which are up to me to decide where and how I apply. Working with her is energizing, uplifting and clarifying. Before meeting her, I had no idea what an Oracle was but her Oracle on Demand service has a ROI that's difficult to quantify...time & money savings and decisions accuracy. My work with. Christie has also given me much more confidence in my own intuition's accuracy."

- Diane D.

Testimonials

" I was introduced to Christie and her work by a friend of mine. I was really impressed by her ability to read the energy, provide clarity and boost my confidence to forge my new journey. I definitely recommend to anyone to connect with Christie to tap into her powerful intuitive insights, be challenged in a way you may not have been challenged before and discover what's truly possible.

- Stephan V.

The Power to Rise

A Modern Evolution of Napoleon Hill's Timeless Wisdom

By Christie Russ

CENTER FOR CREATORS

ISBN: 979-8-9921378-0-4 (Hardcover) | 979-8-9921378-1-1 (Paperback)

Published by:
Center for Creators

This book is intended for informational and inspirational purposes only. The author assumes no responsibility for any actions taken based on the content of this book.

Cover Design: Christie Russ

Editor: Diane Doster

First Edition: January 2024
Printed in the United States of America

Disclaimer

The information provided in this book is for educational and inspirational purposes only. It is not a substitute for professional advice, including but not limited to legal, financial, medical, or therapeutic guidance. The author and publisher assume no responsibility for any actions, decisions, or outcomes resulting from the use of this book's content. Readers are encouraged to consult licensed professionals for advice tailored to their specific circumstances.

This book is based on the author's personal experiences, memories, and opinions. Some names, identifying details, and events have been changed to protect the privacy of individuals. Any resemblance to actual persons, living or dead, is purely coincidental. The author and publisher make no representations or warranties about the accuracy or completeness of any information in this book. The content is intended for informational and inspirational purposes only, and no liability is assumed for any interpretations or outcomes based on the content of this book.

"Whatever the mind can conceive and believe, it can achieve."

-Napoleon Hill

To my daughters,

You are my greatest inspiration, my deepest motivation, and the unwavering light that guides me every single day.

Your laughter has the power to heal even my heaviest moments. Your strength is a testament to the resilience and courage within you, inspiring me to rise above every challenge and never back down. And your love—pure, unconditional, and boundless—teaches me what it truly means to be connected to something greater than myself.

Everything I do, every step I take, is rooted in my love and gratitude for you. You are the reason I dare to dream bigger, to push past my own limits, and to become the best version of myself—not just for me, but for you.

I am endlessly proud of the extraordinary people you are becoming. You are my heart, my joy, and my most profound blessing. Being your mother is the greatest gift of my life, and I thank the Universe every day for choosing me to walk this journey with you.

With all my love,
Mom

Disclosure Statement

This book is a deeply personal exploration of my journey, inspired by profound experiences, timeless wisdom, and transformative moments of growth. It draws heavily on the enduring principles of success first articulated by Napoleon Hill in *Think and Grow Rich*. These principles—such as desire, faith, persistence, and imagination—serve as the foundation upon which I've built my own life strategies and personal philosophies.

While the insights, stories, and strategies shared within these pages are authentically mine, they are presented in the context of Hill's timeless wisdom, reinterpreted through my experiences and adapted to modern contexts. This book is not a replacement for Hill's work but a continuation of his legacy, filtered through the lens of my unique perspective.

In creating this book, I have embraced leading-edge tools and technologies to enhance the clarity and precision of my writing. In some sections, AI-assisted tools have been utilized to refine language and organize concepts, ensuring the content aligns seamlessly with my vision and purpose.

Thank you for allowing me to share this journey with you. My hope is that these words, inspired by both Hill's wisdom and my life's lessons, ignite the spark within you to embrace your own power to rise.

With gratitude and purpose,
Christie Russ

Table of Contents

Part 2: The Forces That Drive Achievement

Part 3: Rising Above

Introduction: The Call to Rise

Every great transformation begins with a spark—a moment when the life you've been living no longer feels like enough. It's a quiet knowing, a whisper deep within your soul, urging you to rise, to break free from limitations, and to step boldly into the life you were born to live.

This book is your invitation to answer that call.

It is a guide for those who refuse to settle, for those who are ready to harness the principles of greatness and unlock their highest potential. Inspired by Napoleon Hill's timeless teachings, *Power to Rise* goes beyond surface-level success. It's about aligning your mind, body, and soul with a vision so powerful, it transforms not only your life but the world around you.

The path won't always be easy. Growth never is. It demands that you step out of your comfort zone, confront your fears, and embrace the unknown. But it is in these moments—when you feel stretched and challenged—that your greatest breakthroughs are born.

This journey isn't just about achievement, it's about evolution. It's about discovering who you truly are when you let go of doubt, fear, and resistance. It's about pushing the boundaries of what's possible and creating a life that uplifts and inspires you every single day.

You don't need to wait for permission or validation. You don't need to wait until tomorrow or someday. The time is now.

Are you ready to think bigger? To dream bolder? To thrive beyond limits?

This is your moment. Let's begin.

Chapter 1

Ignite Desire - The Spark That Fuels All Great Achievements

"The starting point of all achievement is desire."
– Napoleon Hill

Every great achievement in history begins with one thing: desire. Not a fleeting thought, not a casual wish, but a deep, burning desire—a force so strong that it shapes your thoughts, actions, and ultimately, your reality. Napoleon Hill understood this better than anyone when he wrote *Think and Grow Rich*. His words have inspired millions, offering a roadmap to success that has stood the test of time.

Hill wasn't talking about the kind of desire that fades when obstacles arise. He was talking about the kind that fuels you through adversity, the kind that refuses to be extinguished. Desire, he said, is the emotional force that transforms a dream into a goal and a goal into reality.

In today's world, this principle is more relevant than ever. We live in an era of constant distractions—a world where our attention is pulled in a thousand directions, and our dreams are often silenced by the noise of everyday life. Yet, it is desire that cuts through this chaos. It is the compass that guides us toward what truly matters, the fire that propels us forward when the path is unclear. For me, the principle of desire isn't just a concept, it is the foundation upon which I rebuilt my life.

A Moment That Changed Everything

There are moments in life that change everything—moments that shatter the illusion of who we've been and demand we confront who we truly are.

These are the moments that break us open, forcing us to see with startling clarity what we've allowed, what we've lost, and what we are no longer willing to endure. For me, that moment came on what should have been an ordinary day.

The sun hung high over Angel Stadium, casting a golden glow over the excitement of a family outing. The air buzzed with the hum of the crowd, the faint scent of hot dogs and popcorn mingling with the warmth of the California afternoon. My daughters' laughter rang out, bright and innocent, cutting through the noise. For the first time in what felt like forever, I allowed myself a flicker of peace—a fragile glimmer of the woman I used to be, a woman who felt joy, ease, and lightness.

But peace is a fleeting thing when you live in a world built on eggshells. In an instant, with just a few whispered words, that moment was obliterated. My husband leaned in close, his voice low but sharp, his words slicing through me like a blade honed for this exact purpose. The comment was calculated and deliberate, a cruel reminder of how small he wanted me to feel, how much he enjoyed keeping me tethered to a reality that wasn't my own.

It wasn't the first time. His words had chipped away at me for years, stripping me of my confidence, my stability, and my sense of self. Each barb had left its mark, a scar invisible to the world but etched deeply into my soul. But this time, something was different. This time, something inside me cracked wide open.

I excused myself quickly, my heart pounding and my breath shallow, desperate to keep my daughters from noticing the tears welling in my eyes. My legs felt heavy as I began climbing the ramps of the stadium, each step harder than the last as the weight of two decades bore down on me. Two decades of silencing my dreams, of walking on edge, of shrinking into a version of myself so small I barely recognized her. The air grew thinner the higher I climbed, my chest tight with the burden of every insult, every unspoken word, every moment I had handed over my power.

By the time I reached the open air, the tears I had been holding back came in waves, hot and relentless. I stood there, staring out over the city, the hum of the stadium fading into the background as my mind raced with the echoes of all the years I had endured.

Every cruel word, every moment of doubt, every part of myself I had sacrificed came rushing forward. The sheer weight of it threatened to crush me.

And then, amid the chaos, something extraordinary happened. A single thought erupted inside me like a thunderclap cutting through a storm: Fuck You! *I'm done.*

It was a roar inside—raw, primal, and undeniable. It echoed through the deepest parts of me, shaking loose every fear, every excuse, and every shred of doubt I had clung to for so long. For the first time in years, I felt a clarity so sharp it was almost blinding. This wasn't just about leaving a marriage. This was about reclaiming my life, who I was and my power.

The thought wasn't born out of anger—it was born out of necessity. It wasn't about survival anymore; it was about creation. *I will rise from this.* I didn't just want freedom, I demanded it. I wanted to become a woman my daughters could look at and see strength embodied. I wanted them to know what resilience looked like. I wanted them to see that no matter how far you fall, you can always rise again.

Standing on that ramp, the air crisp and biting against my cheeks, I felt something awaken in me. It was a fire—not a flicker, but an inferno. It burned brighter and hotter with every beat of my heart, consuming every ounce of doubt, shame, and fear that had held me captive. I could feel it in every cell of my body, radiating outward, filling me with an energy I had never known before.

It wasn't hope—it was determination. It wasn't longing—it was resolve. And it wasn't polite. It was raw, unapologetic, *F.U.* energy coursing through my veins, whispering with unshakable certainty: This isn't the life I want, *I deserve more, and I will not stop until I make it happen.*

That moment on the ramp wasn't just a breaking point, it was a rebirth. It was the moment I chose *me.* The moment I saw my worth with clarity so vivid it felt as though the Universe itself had handed me a mirror. This wasn't the beginning of an ending—it was the ignition of a new beginning.

With every ounce of that fire inside me, I vowed that I would not just rebuild my life, I would reinvent it. I would rise higher, stronger, and freer than I had ever imagined.

Why Desire is the Foundation of Success

Napoleon Hill believed that desire is the starting point of all achievement because it is the force that keeps us moving forward, even when the odds are stacked against us. Without it, our dreams remain just that—dreams. But with it, we can overcome obstacles, push through fear, and turn even the most audacious goals into reality.

Desire fuels persistence. It's what compels us to take risks, to try again after failure, and to keep going when everything in us wants to quit. It turns vague hopes into clear visions and visions into plans. And most importantly, it gives us the courage to act.

For me, desire was the only thing that kept me moving forward after that moment at Angel Stadium. I didn't have a plan. I didn't know what the future would look like. All I knew was that I couldn't stay where I was. That clarity—that burning desire— became my anchor. It gave me the strength to make decisions I had avoided for years and the courage to step into a future that felt terrifying and uncertain.

Desire in Today's World

In the age of endless scrolling, constant notifications, and curated perfection on social media, desire is more crucial than ever. It's easy to lose ourselves in the noise, to compare our lives to the highlight reels of others and feel like we're falling short. We set goals based on what we think we should want, not what truly resonates with us, and wonder why we feel unfulfilled.

Desire is the antidote to this confusion. When you have a burning desire, distractions lose their power. Your focus sharpens, your energy aligns, and suddenly, the opinions of others no longer matter. For me, desire was what cut through the noise of self-doubt and external judgment. It gave me clarity in a world that thrives on confusion.

The Six Steps

Napoleon Hill's six-step method for cultivating desire became my guide during this transformative period of my life. These steps are timeless, effective, and surprisingly simple:

1. **Define Your Goal Clearly**

   The first step is clarity. Vague desires lead to vague results. For me, the goal was clear: to reclaim my identity, rebuild my confidence, and create a life of strength and purpose that my daughters could look up to.

2. **Determine What You'll Give in Exchange**

   Every goal comes with a cost. Whether it's time, energy, or letting go of old habits, success requires sacrifice. For me, it meant leaving behind the false security of my marriage and embracing the uncertainty of starting over.

3. **Set a Deadline**

   A goal without a deadline lacks urgency. I didn't have the luxury of waiting for the "perfect time." My transformation began the moment I decided to act.

4. **Write It Down**

   Hill believed in the power of writing down your goals. Seeing my desires on paper made them feel tangible and real. It was a daily reminder of the life I was working toward.

5. **Visualize and Affirm Daily**

   Visualization was one of the most powerful tools I used. Every morning, I closed my eyes and imagined myself living the life I wanted. I saw myself strong, confident, and free. I repeated affirmations that reinforced this vision, letting myself feel the emotions of success before it arrived.

6. **Take Decisive Action**

   Desire without action is just a dream. Every day, I asked myself: *What can I do today to move closer to my goal?* Sometimes the steps were small; other times, they were monumental. But every action fueled momentum.

Your Journey Begins Here

Now it's your turn. Take a moment to reflect on your own life. What is your deepest, most burning desire? What is the one thing you want so badly that it keeps you awake at night? Write it down. Be specific. Imagine what your life will look like when that desire becomes reality. Feel it. Believe it. And then, ask yourself: *What am I willing to give in exchange to bring this dream to life?* Remember, it does not have to feel like a sacrifice. Instead, think of it as offering something that fills you with joy and purpose—a commitment that fuels your passion and aligns with your highest potential.

Desire is the seed of every great achievement. It's the fire that transforms dreams into goals and goals into reality. What will you do with yours? Begin today. Define your desires. Write them down. Visualize them. Act on them. Because when you do, you will discover that the life you've always dreamed of isn't just possible, it's waiting for you.

Affirmations to Strengthen Desire

Repeat these affirmations daily to reinforce your belief in your goals:

1. *I am clear on my desires, and I pursue them with unwavering focus.*

2. *I release all that no longer serves me and embrace the power of my vision.*

3. *Every day, I take steps that align with my highest purpose.*

4. Success flows through me effortlessly, and I embody confidence, strength, and unstoppable power in all I do.

5. *My burning desire fuels my actions and propels me toward greatness.*

Chapter 2

Unshakable Faith - Transform Belief into Breakthroughs

"Faith is the eternal elixir which gives life, power, and action to the impulse of thought."
– Napoleon Hill

Faith is more than belief. It is the unshakable conviction that what you desire is already yours, even before the evidence appears. In *Think and Grow Rich*, Napoleon Hill calls faith the "eternal elixir" because it gives thought the energy to transform into reality. Faith bridges the gap between where you are and where you want to be, empowering you to move forward when doubt threatens to hold you back.

Faith is not a passive state. It is a decision, a discipline, and sometimes, a lifeline. For me, faith wasn't something I stumbled upon, it was something I had to cultivate. In moments when fear loomed larger than hope, faith became my anchor. And it all began during one of the most uncertain times of my life.

A Different Kind of Starting Point

After leaving my marriage, I knew I had stepped into a storm of unknowns. While my decision had been clear in the moment, the aftermath was anything but. I was navigating a life that felt both new and terrifying—raising three daughters, confronting financial instability, and piecing together a vision of who I wanted to become. Faith wasn't something I could afford to have—it was something I needed to survive.

Faith isn't something that arrives all at once. It doesn't sweep in and erase the pain or uncertainty in an instant. Sometimes, it takes time—time to settle, to take root, and to grow. For me, faith didn't come with a flash of clarity. It emerged slowly, quietly, in the rhythm of a ritual that became my lifeline.

Each morning began the same. I would drive them to school. They disappeared through the school doors, and it was then that I could release and let the tears flow and stop having to try and be strong.

By the time I returned home, it felt as though the walls of the house were closing in, amplifying the weight of everything I was trying to hold together. Bills were piled on the counter, unanswered questions circled in my mind, and the overwhelming uncertainty of the future loomed over me. Constantly being reminded of the words my ex left with. "You are 50 years old and have nothing to offer. No one is going to want you; you are going to end up just like your mother." You see, my mother had taken her life at 59. But those words were the most motivating words that had ever been said to me. They gave me strength and absolute clarity as to who he was and that I would never allow anyone, anyone to ever hold me back. I had way too much to offer the world. Again, it was that F.U. energy that fueled my desire.

Every morning, after wiping the tears from my cheeks, I would hit play on Linda Ronstadt. Why her, I'll never know, her voice would fill the room like a balm, and I would begin to move. The first mornings were raw and excruciating. I danced not because I felt like it, but because it was the only thing I could do. My feet shuffled across the floor, my arms moved half-heartedly, and my tears fell freely and I would lose myself. I felt numb— completely and utterly numb. There was no joy, no hope, no connection to the woman I used to be or the life I was trying to rebuild.

And yet, I danced. Every day, it was what I looked forward to. I could lose myself into a world I wasn't understanding at the time. Linda's songs became the rhythm of my grief, her voice the companion I didn't know I needed. The numbness didn't lift overnight.

Over time, something began to shift. It was subtle at first, so faint I almost missed it. A spark of awareness, a flicker of something more. My movements became a little freer, I could begin to feel a smile. The tears still came, but they didn't feel as heavy—they felt like release, like a slow unraveling of everything I had been holding inside.

Weeks passed, and the numbness began to crack. In its place, something softer began to emerge—a quiet sense of connection, a faint whisper of hope. It wasn't loud or overwhelming, but it was there, steady and insistent.

The emptiness that had once consumed me was beginning to be replaced by something warm, something alive. Faith that I was going to be ok, it didn't arrive all at once, but it began to bloom in those moments, fragile and new. It wasn't just faith in the future, it was faith in myself.

I began to see the woman I was becoming, the woman I once was. With every turn, every stretch, I reclaimed pieces of myself I thought I had lost. The tears still came, but they were different now. They weren't just tears of pain, they were tears of gratitude, of release, of knowing that I was going to be okay.

Dancing became my sanctuary. Linda's voice guided me each morning, a steady reminder that I was still here, still moving, still alive. The act itself became a declaration: *I am not giving up. I am not staying numb. I am not letting this defeat me.*

Not is often a word that often feels heavy, filled with resistance or finality. In moments of despair, it can anchor you to a belief: *I cannot do this,* a thought that defines your energy and broadcasts to the universe your belief in your limitations. But at that moment I saw *not* differently. I embraced it as a word of power, a word of choice. *I am not giving up* wasn't just a refusal to quit—it was a proclamation of strength, a fuel that drove me toward change.

This recognition of how we use words—and the energy and emotion we feel when we say them—became my lifeline. When climbing the emotional scale that Esther Hicks so brilliantly describes, you don't leap from despair to joy in an instant. When you're broken, shattered into pieces, the words *I am* can feel too distant, too unattainable. Sometimes, the first step is recognizing what you refuse to feel, what you refuse to be. *I am not staying numb* was my first step. It wasn't joy, it wasn't empowerment, but it was movement. It was a foundation I could stand on, even if it was shaky at first.

Faith doesn't need to be grand or dramatic. Sometimes, it's as simple as putting one foot in front of the other, as subtle as swaying to a song when you feel like collapsing. For me, faith wasn't about knowing how everything would work out, it was about trusting that I could find my way, one step, one morning, one song at a time.

That ritual, those mornings of dancing, became the foundation of my faith.

They reminded me of something profound: that even in the darkest moments, there is always a way forward. It may not come quickly, and it may not come easily, but it will come. You just have to keep moving.

Why Faith is Essential to Success

Faith is the bridge between desire and action. Napoleon Hill believed that without faith, even the most powerful desires would crumble under the weight of doubt. Faith is what gives you the courage to act, the strength to persist, and the resilience to rise after every setback.

When you cultivate faith, you begin to see the world differently. Challenges become opportunities, and setbacks become lessons. Faith doesn't eliminate fear—it transforms it into fuel. It allows you to trust the process, even when the outcome isn't yet visible.

For me, faith became the lens through which I saw my journey. Every time fear threatened to take over, I reminded myself that success wasn't just possible, it was inevitable, as long as I kept moving forward.

Faith in a World of Uncertainty

In today's world, faith can feel elusive. We live in an age of instant gratification, where success is often measured by how quickly results are achieved. Social media bombards us with curated images of perfection, creating a culture of comparison that erodes our confidence. When progress feels slow or setbacks arise, it's easy to lose faith—not just in the process, but in ourselves.

But true faith isn't dependent on external validation. It is an internal knowing, a quiet confidence that remains steady regardless of circumstances. Faith is what allows you to see beyond the noise, to hold your vision steady, and to trust that everything is unfolding exactly as it should.

During the early days of rebuilding my life, faith wasn't something I always felt—it was something I chose. It meant trusting that every small step mattered, even when the bigger picture felt unclear. It meant believing in my ability to create a new life, even when I couldn't yet see the full path.

Cultivating Faith: Napoleon Hill's Method

Napoleon Hill provides a clear framework for building faith, one rooted in repetition, visualization, and aligned action. These steps became the foundation for my own journey and can do the same for yours:

1. **Create a Clear Affirmation**

   o Write down a specific statement of your desire, framed as though it is already achieved.

   o Example: *I am living a life of abundance, joy, and purpose.*

2. **Speak Your Affirmation Daily**

   o Repeat your affirmation aloud twice a day, morning and night, with conviction. Let the words sink in until they feel true.

3. **Visualize Your Success**

   o Spend time each day imagining your desired outcome as though it is already real. Engage all your senses, see the details, hear the sounds, and feel the emotions of success.

4. **Take Decisive Action**

   o Faith without action is empty. Identify one small step you can take today that aligns with your vision and commit to it.

5. **Protect Your Energy**

   o Surround yourself with positivity. Limit your exposure to negativity, whether it comes from others or your own inner dialogue.

Personalization: Build Your Faith Today

Faith is not reserved for the extraordinary—it is available to anyone willing to cultivate it. Take a moment to reflect on an area of your life where you feel uncertain. What would it look like to approach that situation with unshakable faith?

- Write down your vision for what you want to achieve.

- Create an affirmation that reinforces your belief in that vision.

- Spend 5 minutes each day visualizing your success.

- Take one aligned action today, no matter how small.

Faith is a choice you make every day. It is not about eliminating doubt, it is about choosing to act in spite of it. It is about trusting that each step you take is leading you toward the life you desire.

So take the leap. Speak your vision into existence. Act as though your success is already yours. Because when you cultivate faith, you turn your dreams into reality.

Affirmations to Strengthen Faith

1. *I trust and know that everything is unfolding perfectly.*

2. *I am already living a life of success, abundance, and purpose.*

3. *Every action I take brings me closer to my vision.*

4. *I am confident, capable, and aligned with infinite possibilities.*

5. *I walk forward in faith, knowing my dreams are my reality.*

Chapter 3

Rewire Your Mind - The Power of Autosuggestion

"The principle of autosuggestion is the agency of control through which an individual may voluntarily feed his subconscious mind on thoughts of a creative nature or, by neglect, permit thoughts of a destructive nature."

– Napoleon Hill

There is a quiet, yet powerful force working within you at all times: your subconscious mind. It doesn't discriminate between positive or negative thoughts. It simply acts on the instructions it receives. In *Think and Grow Rich*, Napoleon Hill reveals that the principle of autosuggestion is the key to influencing this force, transforming your thoughts into tangible outcomes.

Autosuggestion is the process of feeding your subconscious mind with intentional, focused thoughts. It is how you train your mind to work for you, aligning your beliefs, emotions, and actions with your desires. It turns affirmations and visualizations into more than mere rituals—it makes them tools of transformation.

For me, learning to master autosuggestion was life changing. It became the bridge between faith and action, allowing me to reprogram years of self-doubt and limiting beliefs into a mindset of possibility and empowerment.

The Moment I Realized the Power of My Thoughts

No matter how many steps forward I took, I couldn't silence the nagging voice in my head that whispered, *I'm never going to make it. I have nothing to offer.* People don't like me.

These thoughts felt automatic, they had been hardwired into my mind over years of living in an environment that constantly undermined my confidence.

One morning, after being on edge and snapping at my girls, I thought, *is this who I want to be? A woman who felt like she was losing her mind and the respect of her children*. The answer was clear: Fuck No!. Wanting to change and knowing how to change felt like two very different things.

After I dropped the kids off at school, I sat down with a notebook and wrote, *I am strong. I am capable. I have freakin got this, I am creating a life of joy and abundance*. At first, the words felt hollow, like I was trying to convince myself of something I didn't fully believe. But it was the evolution of going from knowing what I didn't want to knowing what I did want. Evolving from *not* to I Am. I made a commitment to repeat them every day, morning and night, as Napoleon Hill suggested. I said them aloud, even when I didn't feel like it, and visualized the woman I was becoming.

I would tell my girls with confidence and humor; I'm going to fake it till I make it! Embrace who you want to be.

Over time, something remarkable happened. The words stopped feeling like lies. They began to feel like truths. The more I repeated them, the more my actions aligned with the version of myself I was affirming. I started taking bolder steps, communicating more clearly, and pursuing opportunities I once would have avoided. Autosuggestion became the key to transforming not just my thoughts, but my entire reality.

Why Autosuggestion Works

The subconscious mind doesn't reason or question, it simply accepts. It acts on the thoughts and emotions that are most dominant in your mind, whether they serve you or not. This is why autosuggestion is so powerful: it gives you the ability to intentionally plant thoughts that align with your desires.

When you consistently feed your subconscious mind with affirmations, visualization, and belief, those thoughts take root. They influence your emotions, shape your decisions, and ultimately, create the outcomes you experience. It's not magic, it's the result of aligning your inner world with your outer actions.

The Danger of Negative Autosuggestion

Just as autosuggestion can work in your favor, it can also work against you. Negative self-talk, limiting beliefs, and fear-based thinking are forms of autosuggestion that can keep you stuck. Every time you tell yourself, *I'm not good enough,* or *I can't do this,* you're reinforcing those beliefs in your subconscious mind.

For years, I unknowingly fed my subconscious mind with destructive thoughts. I allowed self-doubt to guide my actions and confusion to dictate my decisions. It wasn't until I learned to take control of my inner dialogue that I realized how much power I had been giving away.

Rewriting the Script

In today's world, negative autosuggestions are more prevalent than ever. We are constantly bombarded with messages that tell us we're not enough—not successful enough, not attractive enough, not smart enough. Social media amplifies this effect, creating a culture of comparison that can erode self-worth.

But autosuggestion offers a way to rewrite the script. It allows you to drown out the noise of the world and replace it with thoughts that empower you. It's a daily practice, a commitment to choosing thoughts that align with the life you want to create.

My Hamster Wheel Technique

When I catch myself spinning in thought patterns or stories that I know don't serve me—those loops of limiting beliefs, doubts, or fears—I pause. The first thing I do is acknowledge the awareness itself. I say, *"Wow, I'm so proud of myself for recognizing this!"* I never judge myself for how long the thought has been there or how far I've wandered down that mental rabbit hole. Instead, I celebrate the fact that I've noticed it.

Once I've praised myself, I remind myself that this thought isn't helping me. I take a moment to say, *this thought doesn't feel good. It isn't moving me forward, and it's not aligned with who I want to be.* This acknowledgment is powerful because it shifts the focus from the problem to the solution.

Then, instead of trying to force the thought away—which never works—I redirect. I learned from Abraham Hicks that the best way to break free from a negative thought is to pivot to something completely unrelated, something that makes you feel good instantly. For me, that "something" became humor.

I created a mental image that never fails to make me laugh. I imagine a little hamster furiously spinning on a wheel, running and running, stuck in the same place. In my head, I shout, *"Jump!"* And then the hamster transforms into a flying squirrel, leaping off the wheel with total freedom and joy. The visual is so absurd and funny that it instantly shifts my mood. I can't help but laugh, and suddenly, the silly story or limiting belief I was caught up in feels as insignificant as that hamster wheel.

That visual, that joyful flying squirrel, represents freedom for me. Freedom from thoughts that don't serve me. Freedom from old stories that aren't aligned with the person I'm becoming. It reminds me that those thoughts are just passing narratives— ones I can choose to let go of.

So, I encourage you to find your own "hamster wheel" moment. Create a mental image, a go-to thought, or an idea that makes you laugh and redirects your focus. Let it pull you out of the spiral and remind you that you have the power to shift your perspective. Those crazy conversations in your head don't define you. You get to choose what supports you, and you get to choose freedom.

How to Master Autosuggestion: Napoleon Hill's Framework

Napoleon Hill's method for mastering autosuggestion is simple, yet profound. It involves repetition, belief, and emotional intensity. Here's how you can apply it to your own life:

1. **Create a Clear Statement of Desire**

   o Write down a specific statement that reflects what you want to achieve.

   o Example: *I am earning $500,000 and more a year doing work I love and living a life of purpose and joy.*

2. **Repeat Your Statement Twice a Day**

   o Say it aloud, morning and night, with conviction. Speak as though your goal is already achieved.

3. **Attach Emotion to Your Words**

   o Feel the joy, pride, and gratitude of achieving your desire as you say your statement. Emotion is what makes autosuggestion powerful.

4. **Visualize Your Success**

   o   Close your eyes and picture yourself living the reality you've described. Engage all your senses to make the visualization vivid and real.

5. **Eliminate Negative Thoughts**

   o   Be vigilant about replacing negative self-talk with positive affirmations. When a limiting belief arises, counter it with a statement that affirms your worth and capability.

Personalization: Make Autosuggestion Work for You

Autosuggestion is not a one-size-fits-all practice, it's deeply personal. Take some time to reflect on the thoughts you've been feeding your subconscious mind. Are they aligned with your desires, or are they holding you back?

- Write down one area of your life where you want to see change.

- Create a specific affirmation that reflects the outcome you desire.

- Commit to repeating your affirmation twice a day for 30 days, and notice how your thoughts, emotions, and actions begin to shift.

The words you speak to yourself hold immense power. They shape your beliefs, influence your decisions, and determine the course of your life. By mastering autosuggestion, you can take control of that power and use it to create a reality that aligns with your highest vision.

So start today. Speak your desires into existence. Visualize your success with clarity and conviction. And watch as your inner transformation begins to manifest in your outer world.

Affirmations to Empower Autosuggestion

1. *I am the creator of my reality, and I choose thoughts that align with my highest vision.*

2. *I speak words of power and possibility into my life every day.*

3. *I am already living a life of abundance, purpose, and joy.*

4. *My thoughts, emotions, and actions are perfectly aligned with my success.*

5. *I am capable, confident, and unstoppable.*

Chapter 4

Mastery Through Focus - The Courage to Acquire Specialized Knowledge

"Knowledge is only potential power. It becomes power only when, and if, it is organized into definite plans of action and directed to a definite end."
– Napoleon Hill

True power doesn't come from knowing everything—it comes from mastering what matters most. Specialized knowledge, as Napoleon Hill describes it, is the key to transforming raw potential into realized success. It is the sharp blade that cuts through the noise, focusing your efforts on the areas where your unique skills and *vision* can create the greatest impact. It's not just about learning; it's about becoming.

For me, the principle of specialized knowledge wasn't just a concept—it became a way of life. I didn't just acquire knowledge; I immersed myself in it, pushing boundaries and diving into realms that would stretch my understanding and set me apart. This wasn't a casual exploration. It was an all-consuming commitment to being not just informed, but extraordinary. Having a skill that set me apart from everyone.

Honing My Gift: Mastering the Art of Channeling

The journey began with a question that haunted me: *How can I serve at the highest level?* Channeling was already a skill I had used to guide others, but I knew there was more. I didn't want to be just another intuitive voice in the world. I wanted to become a master—a channeler so precise, so aligned, that every insight I offered would create profound transformation. I knew I was here to guide people to their highest good for the highest good of humanity. That I was going to uplift and inspire millions of lives and that was going to have an exponential impact on the world.

To achieve that, I had to dive deeper than ever before. I immersed myself in energy, consciousness, and alignment. I experimented, practiced, and refined my methods. Every session, every moment of connection, was an opportunity to elevate my craft. I was here for global impact and to collaborate with people on the leading edge that are transforming the world for the highest good.

I challenged myself to go beyond intuition and into precision. I sought to channel not just answers, but the highest truths— insights that could unlock a person's deepest potential and align them with their ultimate purpose. This wasn't about proving my worth; it was about becoming a vessel for the highest good, a guide who could help others step into their power with clarity and confidence.

Channeling became more than a skill—it became an art form. I didn't just practice it; I lived it. And in the process, I became something more than a channeler. I became an Intuitive Business Strategist working with Senior Level Executive and High Achievers. To me, Achievers are people who take action at high level and make things happen on a global level. I knew I was only to work with people who could utilize my insight for profound strategy and growth.

Leading the Future: Blockchain, Tokens, and AI

It was 2017 and while I was mastering channeling, I began having non-stop visions and downloads about technologies I knew nothing about. I had no prior knowledge or education in that field. It overwhelmed me, it inspired and exhilarated me. I had never had such pure thirst for knowledge in one specific area. The reason why I was here and what I was to create was beginning to be very clear. There was something about the rapid evolution of blockchain, cryptocurrency, holograms, artificial intelligence and the metaverse that felt electric. These weren't just tools—they were revolutions waiting to happen. And I didn't want to watch them from the sidelines. I wanted to lead.

I dove headfirst into the world of blockchain, educating myself on the problems it was solving. The mechanics of decentralized systems, the power of tokens, what NFTs were, far beyond the images, how it benefited our financial structures, our supply chain, real estate, the list appeared to be endless. For me, I was recognizing how it could help twenty five percent of the population that is unbanked generate revenue. That was the key of my focus, my why to what I was creating. I wasn't content with surface-level knowledge—I wanted to understand the foundations, the why behind the how. I saw blockchain not just as technology, but as a vehicle for transformation, a way to create systems that were transparent, decentralized, and interoperable.

Then there was AI. The possibilities it presented were limitless—streamlining processes, enhancing creativity, and amplifying human potential. I explored how artificial intelligence could integrate with my intuitive work, how these two leading-edge technologies could intersect to create something entirely new. This wasn't just learning, it was innovation.

I didn't stop at understanding; I applied. I created. I envisioned platforms where I could incorporate my channeling with tokens that could incentivize growth, where blockchain could foster trust. Where AI could be consciously programed and I could integrate my channeling to personalize transformation that would guide people to their highest good for the highest good of humanity on an accelerated path. I wanted to be on the leading edge, I knew this was the future. And I didn't just want to keep up with the future—I wanted to shape it. And then I created it.

Center for Creators, the Convergence of Personal Evolution and Blockchain, Conscious AI, Digital Assets, Streaming Holograms and the Metaverse. In 2021 I created and launched the CFC token. The first post I made on Twitter announcing my vision of Center for Creators went viral and my token after two weeks of launch was in the top 1% of tokens out of 9300 tokens on the XRP Ledger. Within less than one month of that I was brought in by the University of Arkansas, Blockchain Center of Excellence as a Mentor and as a use case provider for the company I had formed, Center for Creators. No college degree, completely self-taught. And one of the leading Blockchain schools in the world wanted me. It was beyond surreal.

Why Specialized Knowledge is Essential

Napoleon Hill was clear: generalized knowledge might make you well-informed, but specialized knowledge makes you invaluable. It's not about being a jack-of-all-trades—it's about being a master of one (or a few). Specialized knowledge allows you to create impact, to solve problems that no one else can solve, and to bring something unique to the table.

In my journey, specialized knowledge wasn't just a tool—it was a transformation. It gave me the clarity to see where I could make the greatest difference and the confidence to act on it. It became the foundation for everything I've built.

Pioneering the Intersection of Intuition and Innovation

What makes specialized knowledge so powerful is its ability to intersect disciplines. For me, the blend of intuitive mastery and technological expertise became my superpower. On one side, I was working deeply with individuals, helping them align with their purpose and unlock their highest potential. On the other, I was building systems that could scale transformation, using blockchain and AI to create platforms that served communities and elevated consciousness.

This intersection wasn't accidental—it was intentional. Specialized knowledge doesn't limit you; it expands you. It allows you to connect seemingly unrelated fields, creating opportunities that others can't see. It's where intuition meets innovation, where the personal becomes the universal.

The Courage to Push Boundaries

Acquiring specialized knowledge is rarely comfortable. It demands stepping into the unknown, questioning your assumptions, and embracing the challenges that come with growth. There were moments when the learning curve felt insurmountable, pushing me so far out of my comfort zone that it was almost unbearable.

I remember times when the sheer complexity of blockchain technology or the rapid advancements in AI made my head spin—literally. I would dive so deeply into the material that I had to stop, feeling physically overwhelmed, sometimes even nauseous. It was as though my mind was stretching beyond its limits, processing a language entirely new to me, new to most.

I went against the norm, facing constant doubt from people who didn't understand blockchain. Their linear thinking, backed by no real knowledge, trying to discourage me, sometimes almost making me feel crazy that I had no idea what I was talking about. But I knew, with every ounce of my being, that blockchain was the future—and I was determined to be at the forefront of this leading innovation.

Over and over, people told me how wrong I was. The biggest claim? "We'll never see this in our lifetime." Not one person fully supported or even understood what I saw. There were no videos to learn from, no simple guides to follow. I had to dive and conduct my own deep research, uncovering the brilliance of blockchain technology.

What fascinated me wasn't cryptocurrency—that was just the bonus. It was the different blockchain technologies, the real-world problems they solved, the use cases, and the partnerships already implementing this revolutionary system. Yet, so few people understood this. Most were narrowly focused on the surface: cryptocurrency alone.

Instead of resisting the discomfort, I chose to see it differently. I recognized those moments as proof of growth, evidence that I was pushing boundaries and expanding my capacity. The discomfort wasn't a sign to stop, it was a sign I was exactly where I needed to be.

I refused to settle for surface-level understanding. Every question, every challenge, became an opportunity to refine my skills and expand my vision. I embraced the discomfort because I knew it was the gateway to breakthroughs. With each step forward, I felt myself moving closer to the edge—the place where transformation happens, where the impossible becomes possible.

This was the courage it took: to lean into the unknown, to push through discomfort, and to trust that every overwhelming moment was shaping me into the person capable of achieving the extraordinary.

Cultivating Specialized Knowledge: Napoleon Hill's Method

Napoleon Hill offers a timeless framework for mastering specialized knowledge. Here's how you can apply it to your own life:

1. **Define Your Area of Mastery**

   o Ask yourself: What specific skill or knowledge will allow me to create the greatest impact?

   o For me, it was channeling for the highest purpose and continuing to understand blockchain and AI technologies.

2. **Seek Out the Best Resources**

   o Identify mentors, courses, books, and communities that align with your goals.

   o Surround yourself with people and tools that challenge you to grow.

3. **Immerse Yourself in Practice**

- Knowledge becomes power only when applied. Use what you learn to create, innovate, and contribute.

- Whether channeling for a client building on the blockchain or designing systems with AI, every action reinforced my expertise.

4. **Embrace Lifelong Learning**

- Specialized knowledge isn't static—it evolves. Commit to growing alongside your field and adapting as new opportunities emerge.

5. **Integrate Knowledge Across Disciplines**

- Look for ways to combine your skills, creating unique solutions and opportunities.

- My work became most impactful when I blended intuition with innovation.

Personalization: Your Path to Mastery

Take a moment to reflect on your unique path. What specialized knowledge would set you apart? Write down one area where you want to grow and create a plan to acquire and apply that knowledge.

- Identify one subject or skill to focus on for the next six months.

- Research the best resources, mentors, or communities to guide you.

- Dedicate time each week to learning and applying what you've gained.

Specialized knowledge is the foundation of transformation. It's what allows you to create impact, to innovate, and to lead. By committing to mastery, you unlock doors that others can't even see.

So, ask yourself: *What do I need to know to create the life I desire?* Learn it. Apply it. Master it. Because when you do, you don't just keep up with the future—you define it.

Affirmations to Empower Specialized Knowledge

1. *I am a master of my craft, continually growing and evolving in my expertise.*

2. *I seek and apply knowledge that aligns with my highest vision and purpose.*

3. *I am fearless in exploring new ideas and technologies that amplify my impact.*

4. *Every day, I expand my skills and refine my mastery.*

5. *I stand at the leading edge, shaping the future with my unique knowledge and vision.*

Chapter 5

Create Your Future - The Magic of Imagination

"The imagination is literally the workshop wherein are fashioned all plans created by man."
– Napoleon Hill

Imagination is where it all begins. It's the space where dreams are born, where ideas take shape, and where the unseen becomes possible. In *Think and Grow Rich*, Napoleon Hill calls imagination "the workshop of the mind," a place where creativity transforms desire into plans and plans into reality. It is through imagination that we connect with our deepest potential, visualize our grandest visions, and bring them to life.

For me, imagination is not just a concept—it's a practice. It's where I have created everything that matters in my life, a sacred space where my visions have turned into tangible realities. Imagination isn't about wishing or hoping. It's about entering a realm of creation so vividly that you can see, feel, and know the reality of what you're building before it even exists in the physical world.

Entering the Plateau of Creation

One of the most profound ways I've harnessed the power of imagination is through guided visualization—a practice that takes me beyond the boundaries of the physical world. In these moments, I tap into higher consciousness, connect with infinite possibilities, and create from a space of pure alignment and clarity. Each time I enter this practice, it feels as though I'm stepping into a space where everything is possible and where creation flows effortlessly.

I begin each visualization seated comfortably, my feet flat on the ground, either indoors in a serene, quiet space or outdoors, surrounded by the hum of nature. I close my eyes, allowing the outside world to fade away as I bring my awareness inward. The first sensation is one of grounding. I imagine roots unfurling from the soles of my feet—thick, strong, and alive with energy. These roots grow rapidly, weaving their way down through the soil, deeper and deeper, until they reach the core of the earth itself.

The sensation is tangible. I can feel the cool density of the earth as the roots dig in, going directly down to the core of the earth. As I breathe slowly—inhaling deeply through my nose and exhaling softly find out through my mouth—I become part of the earth's rhythm. With each breath, I visualize a soft, spiraling energy beginning to rise from the core of the earth, traveling up through the roots to the bottom of my feet. The energy is alive, almost pulsating, as it flows toward me. Colors of the energy change and I just go with the flow of what I've been shown that day. It reaches the soles of my feet and begins its gentle ascent into my body.

The energy is not just a color—it's a presence. It carries with it a profound sense of calm, stability, and unconditional love. I can feel it as though it's touching every fiber of my being. It moves slowly, deliberately, filling every cell with its nurturing warmth. My legs feel anchored and steady, my chest opens as the energy rises, and my entire being is enveloped in serenity. I feel my heart swell with confidence and my mind quiets, allowing me to simply *be* in this flow of energy.

Then, as though guided by an unseen force, I begin to feel my energetic self lift. It's not a physical sensation—it's energetic, a lightness that starts at my core and radiates outward. My body becomes weightless, and my awareness begins to expand. It feels as though I am floating effortlessly, rising higher and higher until I am no longer bound by the earth. I find myself in a space so vast it feels infinite. It's like the night sky—deep and endless, dotted with iridescent specks of light that shimmer and dance around me. But this isn't a sky I'm looking at—it's consciousness I'm part of. I can feel the lights flowing through me, separate but one. There's no distinction between where I end and they begin.

In this space there is no fear, no doubt. Only stillness. The gentle waves of higher consciousness flow through me, filling me with a sense of peace so profound it feels otherworldly. I let myself float here, soaking in the serenity, the knowing, the connection to something far greater than myself.

As I surrender to this state, a shift begins. I see myself standing on an iridescent pedestal that glows softly beneath my feet. It feels alive, pulsating gently with the energy of creation. Below me, hands of higher consciousness—strong, supportive, and

54

filled with grace—begin to lift the pedestal higher. I am carried upward, rising through layers of light and energy until I reach a new realm.

The hands of higher consciousness lower and gently place me on my plateau of creation. It is a vast, open field that stretches endlessly in all directions. Untouched, yet waiting. As I step forward, the field begins to transform. With each step, the landscape responds to my presence, coming alive as though it has been waiting for me. The ground beneath my feet grows lush with emerald-green grass, soft and vibrant. Towering trees rise around me, their leaves shimmering in the sunlight. A gentle breeze brushes against my skin, carrying with it the sound of rustling leaves and birds singing.

Every sensation is heightened—the warmth of the sun on my face, the crispness of the air, the steady rhythm of my heart. It feels real, more real than anything I've ever experienced. Each step expands the space, revealing more of its beauty. A stream appears ahead, its water sparkling as it flows. I hop across the stones that line its path, each step steady and sure, until I reach the other side.

On the other side, my vision crystallizes. I see it—the Center for Creators. It's not just an idea anymore, it's alive. The architecture is breathtaking, its colors rich and warm. I hear laughter and conversation, the hum of people coming together with shared purpose and joy. The air buzzes with energy, vibrant and electric. Every detail is vivid, every emotion tangible. I feel excitement, pride, and gratitude radiating through every cell of my being. Every time I go back it's the same beginning experience evolving into the same space that continues to expand with my vision.

This is more than imagination. This is *knowing*. The plateau isn't just a space for dreaming, it's a space for creation. Everything here is real, alive, waiting to be brought into the physical world. When I'm ready to return, I don't leave this place behind. I carry it with me. I pull the energy, the vision, the certainty into the here and now, using it to guide my actions, feeling, knowing, desires and decisions.

The most extraordinary part of this practice is, It's not just for me. I can guide others to their plateau of creation, helping them experience the same euphoric connection to their limitless potential. I can help them feel what it means to create from a place of pure alignment, to step into a reality that already exists and pull it into the now.

Why Imagination is the Workshop of the Mind

Napoleon Hill believed that imagination is where all great achievements begin. It is the space where we visualize solutions to problems, craft plans, and align our thoughts with our desires. Imagination allows us to see beyond our current circumstances, to dream boldly, and to act with purpose.

But imagination isn't passive—it's an active process. It requires intention, focus, and clarity. When you use your imagination deliberately, you create a blueprint for the life you want to build. You see it so vividly that it feels real, and that belief becomes the foundation for action.

Modern Context: Imagination in a Distracted World

In a world filled with distractions, tapping into your imagination is more important than ever. Social media, constant notifications, and the pace of daily life often leave little room for creative thought. But imagination isn't just a luxury, it's a necessity. It's where you step away from the noise and connect with your deepest truths.

Guided visualization is one way to reclaim this space. It's a practice that allows you to shut out the external world and enter a realm of infinite possibility. It reminds you that your thoughts are not limited by your circumstances—that you have the power to create something entirely new, starting with your mind.

Cultivating Imagination: Napoleon Hill's Method

Napoleon Hill outlines two forms of imagination: **synthetic imagination**, which involves combining existing ideas, and **creative imagination**, which taps into higher consciousness for inspiration. Here's how you can cultivate both:

1. **Set Aside Time for Imagination**

   ○ Dedicate 10–15 minutes daily to visualizing your goals. Create a quiet space where you can focus without distractions.

2. **Visualize in Detail**

   ○ Imagine your desired outcome as vividly as possible. See it, feel it, hear it, and experience it as though it already exists.

3. **Anchor Your Imagination with Emotion**

   ○ Attach strong, positive emotions to your vision. Feel the excitement, joy, and gratitude of having already achieved it.

4. **Use Imagination to Solve Problems**

    o   When faced with a challenge, visualize creative
        solutions. Imagine yourself overcoming
        obstacles and succeeding.

5. **Write Down Your Visions**

    o   Capture your ideas and insights on paper.
        Writing reinforces your imagination and gives you
        a tangible plan to act on.

Personalization: Your Plateau of Creation

Everyone has their own plateau of creation—a space where
their imagination flourishes. Take a moment to reflect on yours.
Where do you feel most creative and aligned? Use this space
to visualize your goals, step into your future, and bring it into
the present.

- Create a daily ritual for guided visualization.

- Imagine yourself stepping into your own plateau of
  creation.

- Allow your imagination to guide you, and trust what
  unfolds.

Your imagination is your greatest tool for creation. It allows you to dream beyond your circumstances, to see what others can't, and to bring the impossible into reality. The workshop of your mind is always open—ready for you to create, innovate, and thrive.

So, close your eyes. Enter your plateau of creation. Build the life you desire with vivid clarity and unwavering belief. And when you're ready, bring it into the now.

Affirmations to Empower Imagination

1. *My imagination is limitless, and I create with clarity and purpose.*

2. *I see my vision clearly and feel its reality in every cell of my being.*

3. *I am a creator, turning my dreams into tangible achievements.*

4. *My imagination connects me to infinite possibilities and inspired solutions.*

5. *Every day, I step into my plateau of creation and bring my vision to life.*

Chapter 6

The Blueprint to Achievement - Turning Vision into Action

"The crystallization of desire into action takes place with the help of organized planning."
– Napoleon Hill

Desire gives you the spark, and faith keeps the fire burning, but without action—focused, deliberate action—your dreams remain just that: dreams. Napoleon Hill called organized planning the bridge between desire and achievement, the process by which visions are brought to life and goals are realized. It's not enough to want something or even to believe it's possible. You must plan, act, and refine until your dreams take form.

For me, organized planning wasn't just a skill, it became my salvation. It was the structure that turned chaos into clarity, a roadmap that kept me moving forward when the path ahead felt overwhelming. The moments of faith and imagination were crucial, but it was planning that made those moments tangible. It was through organized planning that I learned to build a life not just on hope but on action.

Turning Chaos into Clarity

After weeks of dancing to Linda Ronstadt, finding faith in the rhythm of her songs, I began to feel something shift inside me. The numbness had faded, replaced by a quiet determination. I knew I was going to be okay. More than ok, I knew I was a strong, intelligent and capable woman that could achieve anything she set her mind to. But knowing wasn't enough, I needed a plan. I deserved a life that felt whole again.

I sat down one evening with a notebook in front of me, the blank page staring back as if asking, *What now?* The truth was,

I didn't know where to start. My life felt like a thousand scattered pieces, and the idea of putting them back together seemed impossible. But then, I remembered something: you don't rebuild all at once. You start with one step, one piece, one plan.

The Power of a Plan

I began with the questions: Why am I here? What is my purpose? *What do I create?* The answer didn't come right away, but I gave myself permission to dream. I wrote down everything that came to mind, no matter how big or small. I wanted to create financial stability for my family, to feel confident in my ability to provide. I wanted to build something meaningful—not just for myself but for others. I wanted to reclaim my voice, my power, and my future.

A Vision with a Purpose

From the moment I first felt the pull to create the Center for Creators, I knew this wasn't just an idea, it was a calling. I understood, with a certainty that came from somewhere beyond myself, that I was here to uplift and inspire the world.

This wasn't about creating a business; it was about creating legacies with global impact.

Center for Creators embodies the convergence of my channeling of the highest pure positive insight and the ability to rise into higher consciousness. Through this elevated perspective, we are now able to reinterpret wisdom on a higher level, gaining fresh insights and new understandings that transcend previous interpretations.

This evolving wisdom merges seamlessly with leading-edge technologies like blockchain, cryptocurrencies, artificial intelligence, streaming holograms, and the Metaverse. Center for Creators is the catalyst for profound personal growth, equipping individuals with the tools to integrate these insights into creating groundbreaking businesses, innovative ideas, and transformative strategies.

The impact extends far beyond the individual, igniting a ripple effect of innovation, consciousness expansion, and legacy creation that shapes a more evolved and connected world.

But this vision didn't come fully formed. It arrived piece by piece, moment by moment, guiding me to build something I had never seen before. The details would often come in quiet moments of reflection, flashes of inspiration that felt more like divine downloads than conscious thoughts. I didn't always know how I would make it happen, but I trusted that each step would reveal itself as I moved forward.

The Plan that Built Vision

Planning didn't come naturally to me at first, especially in an area as vast and unfamiliar as leading-edge technology. Blockchain, AI, and other emerging technologies were completely foreign to me when the vision for Center for Creators first began to take shape. But I knew this was part of the path—part of what I needed to learn and master in order to build the foundation for something extraordinary.

I began with a simple truth: I didn't need to know everything at once. All I needed was the next step.

- **Step 1: Absorbing New Technologies**

  I immersed myself in the world of blockchain, learning everything I could about decentralized systems, tokens, and their potential to revolutionize the way we connect and create. Artificial intelligence became another focus—its ability to amplify human potential felt perfectly aligned with the vision of the Center. I studied, asked questions, sought mentors, and allowed myself to be a beginner.

- **Step 2: Marrying Wisdom and Innovation**
  I knew that technology alone wasn't enough. The heart would be its principles of alignment, energy, channeling and transformation that had stood the test of time. Planning became an act of convergence, weaving together these seemingly disparate elements into a cohesive whole.

- **Step 3: Building the Foundation**
  As the vision became clearer, I created the vision and roadmap. I personalized strategies, immersive experiences, and tools for both individual and collective transformation. I created a plan that focused not only on the end goal but on the foundation required to support it. Each day brought new clarity, each decision a new piece of the puzzle.

A Moment of Breakthrough

One morning, as I reviewed my plans, I noticed something remarkable: the list of "what ifs" that had once paralyzed me had been replaced by a list of actions I had taken. I had created a plan that others respected and wanted to be part of, started pursuing opportunities that aligned with my strengths, and even began laying the foundation for something bigger—a vision for the future that felt both exciting and achievable.

I realized that planning wasn't just about organization, it was about empowerment. Every plan I created, every step I took, reminded me that I was capable. It gave me back my power, my confidence, and my belief in what was possible.

Cultivating Organized Planning: Napoleon Hill's Method

Hill outlines a practical approach to planning that can be applied to any goal, no matter how big or small:

1. **Define Your Goal Clearly**

   o   Be specific about what you want to achieve. Vague goals lead to vague plans.

2. **Break It Into Steps**

   o   Identify the smaller actions needed to reach your goal. Focus on what you can do today, this week, and this month.

3. **Set a Timeline**

   o   Assign deadlines to each step. Timelines create
       urgency and accountability.

4. **Take Action Daily**

   o   Commit to taking at least one action each day
       that moves you closer to your goal.

5. **Be Willing to Adapt**

   o   Plans are not set in stone. Be flexible and adjust
       as needed, but stay focused on your end goal.

6. **Track Your Progress**

   o   Celebrate small wins and reflect on what's
       working. Progress fuels motivation.

Personalization: Create Your Own Plan

Take a moment to reflect on your goals. What is one thing
you've been dreaming of but haven't yet acted on? Use this
framework to create a plan:

- Write down your goal.

- Break it into smaller steps.

- Identify one action you can take today.

- Set a timeline and commit to following through.

Remember, progress isn't about perfection—it's about consistent, intentional action.

Organized planning isn't just about achieving your goals—it's about reclaiming your power. It's about turning dreams into actions, actions into progress, and progress into transformation.

So, what will you create? Sit down with a notebook, map out your vision, and take the first step. Because when you plan with intention, you're not just building a life, you're building a legacy.

Affirmations to Empower Planning

1. *I am the architect of my life, and I create with clarity and purpose.*

2. *Every plan I make brings me closer to my vision.*

3. *I take consistent, intentional steps toward my goals every day.*

4. *My plans are flexible, adaptable, and aligned with my highest purpose.*

5. *I have everything I need to create the life I desire.*

Chapter 7

Decide to Succeed - Mastering the Power of Commitment

"Successful people make decisions quickly and change them slowly. Unsuccessful people make decisions slowly and change them quickly."
– Napoleon Hill

Every transformation begins with a decision. It's not the kind of decision made in passing or with hesitation, but a firm, unwavering choice—a choice that says, *This is the direction I'm going, and nothing will stop me.* Napoleon Hill identified decision-making as one of the most critical principles of success. To him, indecision was the thief of opportunity, while decisive action was the mark of greatness.

For me, learning to make clear, bold decisions was the turning point in building my life, my work, and my vision. The power of decision wasn't just about choosing—it was about committing. It was about trusting that once the decision was made, the path would unfold, and any course corrections could come later.

Deciding to Lead

One of the most pivotal decisions I ever made came during the early stages of creating Center for Creators. The vision was expansive, and the task of bringing it to life felt exhilarating.

I never hesitated. The biggest decision I made was creating the CFC Token, a bold move that proved to others—and to myself—that this vision wasn't just an idea. It was real, tangible, and unstoppable. Creating the token wasn't simply about embracing cutting-edge technology; it was about stepping fully into the role of a leader, claiming the vision for the Center for Creators with absolute certainty.

The vision was expansive, blending my channeling with cutting-edge technology, merging personal transformation with global impact. These weren't just concepts—they were mandates. And while others might have questioned the enormity of the task, I didn't. I knew that hesitation wasn't an option.

This wasn't about "what if." This was about *how*. How could I take this vision and make it happen? How could I ensure that the foundation was strong, the execution seamless, and the belief unshakable?

The decision to create the CFC Token wasn't a step—it was a leap. It was my way of declaring to the world that this was happening. I was building something revolutionary. It was a decision that didn't leave room for doubt because I didn't move forward with the hope of success—I moved forward with the knowledge that success was inevitable.

And that decision changed everything. It wasn't just about moving forward—it was about *how* I moved forward. With clarity. With intention. With unwavering belief behind every action I took.

Why Decision-Making Matters

Napoleon Hill understood that decision-making is more than just choosing a path—it's about committing to it. When you waver, when you second-guess, you drain your energy and undermine your progress. But when you decide with certainty, you align your thoughts, emotions, and actions with your goal.

Decisive people aren't fearless—they're committed. They trust that even if the path isn't perfect, they'll adjust along the way. They know that clarity of decision is what sets them apart from those who hesitate, falter, or wait for the "perfect" moment.

Overcoming the Fear of Choosing Wrong

One of the greatest obstacles to decision-making is the fear of choosing wrong. What if you make a mistake? What if you fail?

For me, this fear was particularly loud when it came to learning new technologies. Blockchain, cryptocurrency, and AI were fields I hadn't studied before, and the idea of diving into them felt overwhelming. But I realized something powerful: indecision was more dangerous than failure.

Failure, at least, taught you something. It gave you feedback, direction, and clarity. Indecision, on the other hand, kept you stuck in a cycle of doubt, robbing you of the chance to learn, grow, or pivot.

So, I made a decision: I would embrace the role of a student. I would commit to learning, to making mistakes, to trusting that every step forward—even the missteps—would bring me closer to my goal.

A Modern Perspective on Decision

In today's fast-paced world, decision-making feels harder than ever. The endless flow of information, the pressure to make the "right" choice, and the fear of judgment can paralyze even the most ambitious individuals.

But the truth is, the longer you wait to decide, the more opportunities you miss. Success doesn't come to those who hesitate—it comes to those who choose.

The key isn't making perfect decisions, it's making purposeful ones. It's trusting yourself enough to choose and knowing that every choice moves you forward, even if it's not immediately clear how.

A Moment of Bold Decision

One of the most defining moments in building Center for Creators came when I was faced with a choice: continue refining the vision or take action, even though the details weren't perfect.

The perfectionist in me wanted to wait, to polish every aspect until it gleamed. But the leader in me knew better. The time for action was now. The choice was simple: step forward or stay still.

I chose to step forward. And with that decision came a flood of momentum. New opportunities appeared, connections were made, and the vision began to take shape in ways I couldn't have predicted. The lesson was clear: clarity comes through action, not hesitation.

Cultivating the Power of Decision

Napoleon Hill's framework for decision-making offers timeless wisdom that can guide anyone ready to take bold action:

1. **Trust Your Intuition**

   o Decisions are often made with incomplete information. Trust your inner guidance to lead you.

2. **Commit Fully**

   o Once you've made a decision, act on it with conviction. Indecision weakens momentum.

3. **Set Deadlines**

   o Give yourself a timeline for making decisions. Clarity comes when you eliminate endless deliberation.

4. **Be Decisive, Not Perfect**

   o Understand that no decision is flawless. Focus on progress, not perfection.

5. **Learn from Your Choices**

o   Every decision, whether it succeeds or not, teaches you something valuable. Use each lesson to refine your path.

Personalization: Make Your Bold Choice

Take a moment to reflect on an area of your life where you've been hesitating. What decision have you been putting off, and why? Write it down.

Then ask yourself:

- What's the worst that could happen if I choose wrong?

- What's the best that could happen if I choose right?

- What step can I take today to move forward?

Trust yourself. Choose boldly. And know that every decision brings you closer to your highest purpose.

Decisions shape your life. They define your path, your progress, and your impact. So, ask yourself: *What am I ready to commit to? What bold decision can I make today that will move me forward?*

Make the choice. Step into it fully. Because when you decide with clarity and conviction, you unlock a power that will carry you farther than you ever imagined.

Affirmations for Empowered Decision-Making

1. *I trust myself to make bold, purposeful decisions.*

2. *Every decision I make brings me closer to my vision.*

3. *I release the fear of failure and embrace the power of action.*

4. *My clarity and conviction guide me to success.*

5. *I am decisive, resilient, and aligned with my highest purpose.*

Chapter 8

The Relentless Edge - Harnessing the Power of Persistence

"Victory is always possible for the person who refuses to stop fighting."
– Napoleon Hill

Persistence is the quiet force that transforms doubt into confidence, obstacles into opportunities, and visions into reality. It's the unshakable determination to keep moving forward, no matter how many challenges or doubts arise. For me, persistence wasn't just a tool—it was the foundation of everything I built.

When I chose to go all in as an intuitive business strategist, targeting senior executives, the voices of doubt came from all directions.

"Are you crazy? They're going to think you've lost your mind!"
"That demographic won't take you seriously."
"They might even attack your mental stability—what if people start saying you're insane?"

My friends weren't trying to discourage me out of malice; they were genuinely concerned. But I knew better. I trusted my vision and my ability to connect with those who were ready to tap into something deeper. Senior executives and successful leaders often operate with an awareness of something greater, even if they don't fully understand it. I knew I could offer them a safe space to explore that connection.

The Decision to Persist

Choosing this path meant going against everything people told me. It wasn't just a career decision; it was a declaration of who I was and the work I was meant to do.

I joined a private executive club, walking into the room with confidence and introducing myself as an intuitive business strategist. At first, I wondered how people would react, but something amazing happened.

The word "intuitive" stood out, but only to those who were ready. It was as though a silent filter was in place, revealing the exact people I was meant to connect with. These were the ones who paused, leaned in, and asked, "Tell me more about that." Those were the conversations that mattered, and those were the people I shared my truth with.

Each day, I prepared myself for this role with intention. I dressed the part, walking out the door in my best business dress and high heels, repeating to myself, *fake it till you make it*. But deep down, I wasn't faking it—I was aligning with the reality I wanted to create. I was embracing the strength of my femininity and being bad ass bitch.

Manifesting My Vision

Persistence isn't just about enduring; it's about creating. As I stayed consistent in showing up for my vision, the Universe began to meet me halfway. Opportunities appeared that felt almost magical, but I knew they were the result of my unwavering focus and commitment.

One of the most defining moments came when I was invited to a private event at Angels Stadium, showcasing businesses that hosted VIP suites. Walking into the vast stadium that evening felt surreal. It was intimate, with only about 100 guests in attendance, but the energy was electric.

As my friend and I explored, we asked if we could step onto the field and touch home plate. It felt symbolic, standing where so many dreams had been realized. And then, the moment happened.

I turned from home plate and looked up at the massive stadium scoreboard. There it was—my name in lights, displayed alongside the names of the companies represented at the event. My friend had orchestrated the surprise, and in that moment, the enormity of it all hit me.

Full-Circle Magic

Years later, a dear friend reflected on that unforgettable night at Angel Stadium and asked a question that stopped me in my tracks.

"Do you see it?" she said, her voice filled with awe. "You went from breaking down at Angel Stadium to breaking through at Angel Stadium."

The weight of her words hit me like a tidal wave. She was right. The very place where I had once crumbled under the weight of doubt, pain, and uncertainty—the place where I had reached my breaking point—had transformed into the stage where I stood fully in my power.

Angel Stadium wasn't just a location; it was a symbol of my journey. It was the backdrop of my despair and the canvas of my triumph. What began as a moment of heartbreak had come full circle, evolving into a moment of breathtaking fulfillment.

The Universe has a way of weaving its magic, connecting moments in ways that defy logic. That field, where I had once climbed its ramps with tears streaming down my face, became the place where I saw my name in lights and stood surrounded by people who celebrated me. It wasn't just a coincidence, it was a manifestation of every ounce of persistence, belief, and unwavering determination I had poured into my journey.

The path to that moment wasn't smooth. It was filled with twists, challenges, and moments when the voices of fear and doubt tried to take the lead. But I refused to let them define me. I refused to let the fears of others dictate my choices, and I refused to let my own insecurities hold me back.

Angel Stadium taught me that life isn't just about breaking down, it's about breaking through. It's about trusting that the moments of pain and struggle are shaping you, preparing you for something extraordinary. And when you keep moving forward, when you refuse to give up, the Universe responds with a masterpiece—a full-circle moment that reminds you of the power you've always had within.

The Lessons of Persistence

Persistence isn't about never facing challenges—it's about choosing to rise every time you're knocked down. It's about holding onto your vision with unwavering determination, even when the world tells you to let go.

Here's what I've learned about cultivating persistence:

1. **Trust the Process**

    o The path won't always be clear, but trust that every step forward matters. Even the setbacks are part of the journey.

2. **Stay True to Your Vision**

o   Don't let the doubts of others dictate your actions. You know your path better than anyone else.

3. **Celebrate the Small Wins**

   o   Recognize and honor every milestone, no matter how small. Each one is proof that you're moving closer to your breakthrough.

4. **Embrace Challenges**

   o   Challenges aren't roadblocks; they're opportunities to grow stronger and more resilient.

5. **Revisit Your "Why"**

   o   When the road gets tough, reconnect with the deeper purpose behind your vision. Let it fuel your persistence.

To help you cultivate your own persistence and create your full-circle moments, here are practical tools:

- **Journaling Exercise**: Write about a time you overcame a challenge and how it shaped you. Reflect on how that strength can guide you now.

- **Visualization Practice**: Imagine your breakthrough moment in vivid detail. See it, feel it, and let it inspire your daily actions.

- **Micro-Goals**: Break your larger goals into smaller, actionable steps. Focus on one step at a time to maintain momentum.

- **Resilience Routine**: Create a daily practice—whether it's meditation, affirmations, or exercise—that helps you stay grounded and focused.

- **Anchor Affirmation**: Repeat this mantra when persistence feels hard:
  I have faced challenges before, and I will overcome this too. Every step forward is creating my breakthrough.

Persistence is the bridge between where you are and where you want to be. It's the quiet strength that keeps you moving forward, even when the path feels uncertain.

What full-circle moment is waiting for you? What vision deserves your unwavering commitment?

Keep going. Trust your journey. Because one day, you'll find yourself standing in the very place where it all began, transformed and triumphant, and you'll know that you made it.

Affirmations for Persistence

1. *I trust my vision and move forward with unwavering determination.*

2. *Every challenge I face strengthens my resolve and brings me closer to my goals.*

3. *I celebrate progress, knowing that persistence leads to breakthroughs.*

4. *I align my actions with my purpose, and the Universe supports my journey.*

5. *I am resilient, unstoppable, and creating the reality I deserve.*

Chapter 9

Elevate Your Circle - The Power of the Mastermind

"No two minds ever come together without thereby creating a third, invisible, intangible force, which may be likened to a third mind." – Napoleon Hill

Napoleon Hill's principle of the Mastermind is about more than collaboration; it's about creation. When minds come together in harmony, the synergy of their collective energy generates something far greater than the sum of its parts. It's not just about solving problems, it's about creating possibilities, accelerating momentum, and expanding the boundaries of what's achievable.

The term "mastermind" has often been diluted in modern usage, reduced to mere networking or casual brainstorming sessions. However, when I speak of a Mastermind, I embrace the term as Napoleon Hill originally envisioned it—a concept that transcends collaboration and taps into the pure power of creation.

Napoleon Hill's Mastermind principle is about the convergence of minds working in harmony, generating an exponential force that far surpasses what any individual could achieve alone. It's not simply about solving problems or pooling resources; it's about birthing new possibilities, accelerating momentum, and expanding the limits of what is thought possible. A true Mastermind doesn't just produce answers, sparks innovation and transforms visions into realities.

For me, embracing the Mastermind principle wasn't just a choice, it was a necessity. As an intuitive business strategist and the visionary behind the Center for Creators, I recognized that no great endeavor is achieved in isolation. The synergy of a true Mastermind is what fuels creation at its highest level. I needed to be surrounded by individuals who would not only inspire and challenge me but elevate the entire energy of the work we were doing together. This is the essence of the Mastermind: a dynamic, living force of aligned intentions and shared brilliance, creating outcomes that are nothing short of extraordinary.

Conversations That Shift the Energy

From a young age, I realized the power of conversations. Even as a child, I wasn't drawn to gossip or trivial chatter. I couldn't find joy in conversations about people or things—they felt empty, draining. Instead, I craved something deeper, something that made me feel alive.

It wasn't until years later that I understood why. Eleanor Roosevelt's timeless wisdom captured it perfectly:

"Great minds discuss ideas; average minds discuss events; small minds discuss people."

Those words became a guiding light. They validated the way I had always approached life, gravitating toward conversations that explored dreams, ideas, and the big *whys* behind our actions. I began to notice that the quality of conversations directly impacted the energy in a room. Were these words accelerating momentum or slowing it down? Were they creating something meaningful, or were they reinforcing limitations?

Building My Circle of Brilliance

When I fully stepped into my role as an intuitive business strategist, I knew I needed a space where elevated conversations could thrive—a space where ideas flowed freely, where connection felt effortless, and where energy expanded beyond limits.

This vision became the Dinners for Creators: gatherings intentionally designed as safe spaces, free of ego, agendas, or expectations. These weren't just conversations—they were experiences of higher consciousness.

The energy was undeniable. As each person contributed to the conversation, you could feel the collective vibration rising. It was a current of pure positive energy, flowing through every word, every pause, every shared moment.

The room would transform into something almost otherworldly. It was euphoric—a sense of being completely aligned, not just with the people around you, but with something far greater. The boundaries of possibility dissolved, replaced by an overwhelming knowing that *anything* was achievable.

This wasn't just a discussion; it was an elevation. You could feel it in your body, as though every cell was alive, vibrating with the energy of connection and creation. Ideas didn't just spark, they ignited. Solutions didn't just appear—they unfolded with clarity and precision.

These conversations weren't about talking—they were about *becoming*. They were reminders of what happens when we step into a space of higher consciousness, where the only limit is the one we dare to transcend.

This is the power of elevated conversations: they don't just inspire—they transform. They are the doorway to a life where anything is possible.

The Elevated Conversation

Napoleon Hill understood that the power of the Mastermind lies in the quality of its conversations. When you surround yourself with brilliant minds who align with your values but challenge your thinking, something extraordinary happens.

Ideas ignite. Energy accelerates. Solutions emerge almost effortlessly.

This is the essence of elevated conversation. It's not just about what's said, it's about the energy and intention behind it.

I learned to notice this energy in every interaction. Conversations focused on gossip or complaints felt heavy, stagnant, as though they were pulling everyone down. But conversations centered on ideas and possibilities felt light, electric, and expansive.

Elevated conversations push you to think bigger, act bolder, and align more fully with your purpose. They don't just move you forward, they propel you.

Why the Mastermind Principle Works

The Mastermind principle works because it creates a third mind—a collective intelligence that amplifies creativity, innovation, and momentum. It's not about hierarchy or competition; it's about collaboration.

In a true Mastermind, every member contributes their unique strengths while drawing inspiration and support from the group. This synergy creates a ripple effect, with each idea building on the last, accelerating growth and success for everyone involved.

Tools for Creating Your Own Mastermind

If you're ready to harness the power of the Mastermind, here are some practical steps:

1. **Define Your Purpose**

   o   What do you want to achieve? Be clear about your vision and the type of support you need.

2. **Curate Your Circle**

   o   Seek out individuals who align with your values but bring diverse perspectives and skills.

3. **Foster Trust**

   o   Create a safe space where everyone feels valued, heard, and respected.

4. **Focus on Contribution**

   o   Approach every meeting with the intention to give as much as you receive.

5. **Elevate the Conversation**

- Ask bold questions that inspire creativity and challenge limitations, like "What's the most extraordinary version of this idea?"

Who are the people you need in your circle? Who inspires you, challenges you, and pushes you to think bigger? Take a moment to reflect on the conversations in your life. Are they lifting you up or holding you back? Choose to prioritize dialogue that expands your thinking, aligns with your vision, and creates momentum. Because when you engage in elevated conversations within a Mastermind, you don't just achieve success, you create a legacy.

Affirmations for the Power of the Mastermind

1. *I align myself with brilliant minds who inspire and challenge me.*

2. *Collaboration creates infinite possibilities for success.*

3. *I contribute my unique strengths to a powerful collective force.*

4. *Through elevated conversations, I accelerate my vision and impact.*

5. *The synergy of my Mastermind propels me toward extraordinary success.*

Chapter 10

Your Subconscious Blueprint - Unlock Your Silent Ally

"The subconscious mind is the connecting link." –
Napoleon Hill

Napoleon Hill's principle of the subconscious mind is a cornerstone of personal and professional success. It's the bridge between your thoughts and your reality, tirelessly working to align your external experiences with your dominant internal beliefs. By consciously feeding it empowering, focused thoughts, you can transform your desires into tangible results.

For me, this wasn't just theory, it was life-changing practice. I didn't just want clients to come to me. I wanted them to flow to me with ease, alignment, and purpose. To achieve this, I made a commitment to reprogramming my subconscious mind, day by day, thought by thought.

Manifesting Clients and Flow

Each morning, I carved out time to visualize the life I was creating. I sat quietly, closed my eyes, and pictured clients arriving effortlessly, ready to work, ready to take action, and fully aligned with the transformative work we would do together. I imagined our conversations, their excitement, and the breakthroughs they would achieve.

It wasn't just about the visualization—I paired it with an affirmation that became my mantra:

"I am so happy and grateful now that money comes to me in increasing quantities through multiple sources on a continuous basis."
— Bob Proctor

At first, it felt like I was simply repeating words, but I knew the power of persistence. Every day, I spoke those words with intention, layering them with emotion and conviction. Over time, I began to notice subtle changes. My confidence grew. My belief solidified. And then, the results started to flow.

Clients began appearing, seemingly out of nowhere. Each one was more aligned than the last, ready to dive in and take action. They found me effortlessly—through referrals, chance encounters, and synchronicities that felt almost too perfect to be coincidence. It was as if the Universe had opened a direct line between my intention and their arrival.

Refining the Practice

While the flow was remarkable, I wanted the process to feel even more joyful and expansive. So, I refined my affirmation, personalizing it to align with my highest vision:

"Money and clients flow to me easily and effortlessly, in ways that uplift and inspire my mind, body, and soul."

This shift wasn't just about words—it was about energy. By adding a focus on inspiration and upliftment, I felt even more connected to my work and the clients I was attracting. I didn't just want results; I wanted the journey to feel as incredible as the destination.

Later, I added another element: *"Surprise and delight me."* This phrase became a playful invitation to the Universe, opening the door for unexpected blessings and opportunities. It brought a sense of wonder and excitement to the process, making it feel less like work and more like co-creating with infinite intelligence.

And finally, I added the phrase: *"Or something bigger and better."* This ensured I never limited the possibilities, trusting that the Universe could deliver far beyond what I could imagine.

The Results

The transformation was undeniable. Clients continued to arrive—aligned, motivated, and eager to work together. But it wasn't just about the quantity or even the ease. Each client felt like they had been handpicked by the Universe, perfectly suited for the work we were about to do.

Even beyond my clients, opportunities began to appear in ways that truly surprised and delighted me. Collaborations, invitations to exclusive events, and connections with people who inspired me—it all seemed to flow effortlessly into my life.

It was a profound reminder that when you align your subconscious mind with your desires, the Universe conspires to deliver in ways that often exceed your expectations.

Why It Works

The subconscious mind is the ultimate connector. It doesn't question or analyze—it simply accepts the thoughts and beliefs you feed it. By visualizing your desires with clarity and pairing them with strong emotions, you program your subconscious to seek and create the circumstances that align with those desires.

Napoleon Hill described the subconscious mind as the "connecting link" between our conscious thoughts and infinite intelligence. When you consistently feed it positive, intentional thoughts, it acts like a magnet, attracting the people, opportunities, and experiences you need to bring your vision to life.

Practical Tools for Aligning Your Subconscious

1. **Daily Visualization**

   o   Dedicate 5–10 minutes each morning to vividly imagining your desired outcome. Focus on the details, feel the emotions, and experience it as if it's already happening.

2. **Use Affirmations with Emotion**

   o   Repeat affirmations like Bob Proctor's or your personalized versions. Speak them with conviction and pair them with the emotions of gratitude and joy.

3. **Refine Your Affirmations**

   o   Add phrases that make the process feel uplifting, such as *"in ways that inspire my mind, body, and soul"* or *"surprise and delight me."*

4. **Stay Open**

   o   Use phrases like *"or something bigger and better"* to invite limitless possibilities.

5. **Practice Gratitude**

    ○   End each day by acknowledging what you've manifested. Gratitude amplifies the energy of abundance and keeps the flow strong.

Your subconscious mind is your most powerful ally. It's always working—absorbing your thoughts, shaping your beliefs, and creating your reality. Are you feeding it thoughts of abundance, ease, and joy? Take control. Visualize your desires, affirm your intentions, and align your emotions with the reality you want to create. Trust that your subconscious will bridge the gap between your dreams and your destiny, delivering results in ways that surprise, delight, and uplift you. Because when you align with the power of your subconscious mind, anything is possible—and the flow is effortless.

Affirmations for Subconscious Alignment

1. *I am so happy and grateful now that money and clients flow to me effortlessly in increasing quantities through multiple sources on a continuous basis.*

2. *I attract aligned clients who are ready to take action and transform their lives.*

3. *I open myself to opportunities that surprise and delight me.*

4. *The Universe supports my every intention, always exceeding my expectations.*

5. *I am a magnet for abundance, joy, and success.*

Chapter 11

The Infinite Mind - Broadcasting and Receiving Ideas

"The brain is a broadcasting and receiving station for thought." – Napoleon Hill

The brain's power is limitless. It's not just a tool for logic and reasoning but a conduit for connection to higher frequencies of thought. Napoleon Hill understood this when he described the brain as both a transmitter and receiver of ideas. When you consciously choose to tune into higher frequencies, you open yourself to inspiration, creativity, and profound clarity.

For me, this principle became a guiding force in my life. I've always been driven by a belief that if something is worth doing, it's worth doing with intention and focus. One of the quotes that has shaped my approach to life comes from Eleanor Roosevelt:

"Never allow a person to give you a no who doesn't have the authority to give you a yes."

This wisdom has inspired me to go straight to the top in every area of my life. Whether it's business, relationships, or personal growth, I've always bypassed unnecessary layers, choosing instead to focus my energy on the highest and purest possibilities.

Choosing Higher Consciousness

When I began exploring the art of channeling, I didn't just dip a toe into the water—I dove in headfirst, carrying with me a philosophy that had guided my life for as long as I could

remember: *"Never allow a person to give you a no who doesn't have the authority to give you a yes."* Eleanor Roosevelt's words had always inspired me to go straight to the top, bypassing unnecessary barriers and distractions.

I decided to apply that same principle to channeling. I wouldn't settle for surface-level insights or fragmented connections. I made the deliberate, conscious decision to reach for the highest, purest level of positive consciousness—directly, without hesitation.

This wasn't a casual endeavor. It demanded focus, intention, and the courage to push myself beyond my comfort zone. Each time I tuned into a higher frequency, I could feel the shift. It was as though I was floating higher and higher into something vast, something infinite. The energy was electric yet grounding, alive yet calming. I wasn't just thinking or imagining—I was aligning with something far greater than myself. This energy was so expansive that it did take time for my body to adjust to it. I started to call them energy overloads. As though you plug into an electrical outlet that is more powerful than you. At the time it feels good, but then there is the point where you come down and you are absolutely exhausted from connecting to something your body is not adjusted to. I had never in my life napped and I was now taking four-to-five-hour naps as my body adjusted.

And the insights that came through? They weren't just answers; they were revelations. They guided me, healed me, and uplifted not only my life but the lives of the people I served.

A Defining Moment

One moment stands out—a crossroads in my work that left me feeling uncertain and stuck. No matter how much I analyzed or strategized, clarity eluded me. The doubt was heavy, pressing against my chest, and the noise of overthinking clouded every possibility.

Then I remembered: the answers aren't down here in the chaos. They're up there—in the stillness, in the higher frequencies.

So, I stopped. I sat quietly, closed my eyes, and took a deep breath.

I'm ready for the answer. Show me the next step, I whispered, sending the intention out like a prayer, but with the conviction that it would be answered.

As I focused, I visualized my brain as a receiver, fine-tuning itself to the highest frequency of pure positive consciousness. Each breath felt like a step upward.

I climbed higher and higher, leaving behind the noise of doubt and fear, until I reached a space that felt light and expansive.

And then, it came.

The answer wasn't a booming voice or an elaborate vision. It was a quiet, steady knowing that settled into my entire being. It wasn't just the next step, it was *the* step, the one that made everything else fall into place. It was so simple, so profound, that I couldn't believe it hadn't been clear before. But clarity doesn't live in chaos—it lives in alignment.

Straight to the Top

That moment reaffirmed why I choose to go straight to the top. When you align yourself with the highest consciousness, you bypass everything that distracts and diminishes. You skip the noise, the doubts, the distractions, and go directly to the source of pure clarity and truth.

Just as Eleanor Roosevelt's wisdom had taught me to avoid unnecessary roadblocks in life and business, I applied it to my spiritual practice. Why mess around in the fog when I could rise above it? Why settle for fragments when the whole truth was waiting for me?

Choosing to connect with the highest, purest energy wasn't just about receiving answers—it was about aligning with a level of clarity and purpose that elevated every part of my life.

The Power of Alignment

This practice transformed how I approached not just my work, but my entire existence. By choosing alignment over effort, clarity over chaos, I discovered a flow that made everything feel easier and more profound. Solutions emerged effortlessly. Opportunities I hadn't even imagined appeared as if by magic. And the energy I carried into every interaction was magnetic, uplifting, and transformative.

It wasn't about doing more—it was about *being* more. More aligned, more focused, more connected to the energy that makes everything possible.

Every time I chose to ascend into higher consciousness, the results were undeniable. Answers came faster, opportunities expanded, and I felt deeply aligned with my purpose and path.

Why It Matters

The brain is more than an organ for thought—it's a gateway, a receiver capable of tuning into frequencies far beyond what we experience in our everyday lives. When we consciously choose to align it with the highest energy available, we tap into a limitless well of inspiration, guidance, and possibility.

Eleanor Roosevelt's wisdom reminds us not to waste time on distractions. Napoleon Hill's teachings remind us that the brain is a tool for connection. Together, they form a philosophy for living a life that is not only aligned but elevated.

When you choose to rise, to go straight to the top of consciousness, you bypass everything that holds you back. And in that space, everything becomes possible.

Practical Tools to Harness the Brain's Power

1. **Set Clear Intentions**

   o   Before seeking answers or guidance, define your desired outcome with clarity.

2. **Visualize Ascension**

   o   Imagine yourself climbing higher and higher into pure positive consciousness. Feel the energy of alignment as you reach new levels.

3. **Align Your Thoughts**

   o   Replace doubt and fear with empowering affirmations. Focus on thoughts that reflect your highest potential.

4. **Trust the Process**

- o Let go of forcing solutions and allow the answers to come through naturally.

5. **Stay Open**

- o Be willing to receive insights in unexpected ways. Often, the most profound answers come when you least expect them.

Your brain is more than a tool—it's a gateway to infinite potential. Are you using it to its fullest capacity? Are you aligning with the highest and purest frequencies available to you?

Make the conscious choice to go higher. Set your intentions, trust the process, and align yourself with the energy of clarity and inspiration.

Because when you aim straight for the top—when you choose to bypass the noise and distractions—the possibilities are endless, and the answers you seek will always meet you there.

Affirmations for Elevating Consciousness

1. *I align my thoughts with pure positive consciousness and receive clarity effortlessly.*

2. *I trust my brain to connect me with the highest frequencies of inspiration and creativity.*

3. *I go straight to the source of truth, bypassing doubt and distraction.*

4. *My mind is a powerful receiver of limitless possibilities.*

5. *The answers I seek flow to me with ease, in alignment with my highest good.*

Chapter 12

Awaken Intuition - The Sixth Sense of Success

"The sixth sense is the door to the temple of wisdom." – Napoleon Hill

The sixth sense is the culmination of all other principles—a higher form of intelligence, a direct connection to infinite wisdom. Napoleon Hill describes it as an intuitive faculty that guides decisions, reveals opportunities, and provides answers beyond the reach of logic. It is the quiet knowing, the sudden clarity, the instinctual nudge that defies explanation but feels undeniably right.

For me, embracing the sixth sense wasn't just a practice; it was a transformation. I didn't tiptoe into intuition—I dove in completely. Fully embracing my channeling and intuitive knowing became not just a skill but the essence of who I was and how I moved through the world.

Fully Embracing My Channeling

There was a time when I hesitated to fully step into this gift. The voices of doubt, both external and internal, whispered constantly. *What if I'm wrong? What if people think I'm crazy? What if I'm not ready?*

But the pull was stronger than the fear. I couldn't ignore the undeniable clarity that came through when I channeled, the way answers seemed to appear out of nowhere, perfectly aligned with what was needed. I realized that this wasn't about me—it was about the work I was here to do, the people I was meant to help, and the impact I was called to make.

So, I made the decision: I would stop second-guessing. I would stop filtering. I would fully trust what came through.

A Defining Moment of Trust

I was working with a client who was the co-founder and CEO of a $60 million company. The company was facing challenges, and he was in the process of bringing in a new president—a man he deeply trusted. He spoke about this man with reverence, describing him as a father figure, a savior who would make everything right.

At the time, my gift of channeling and intuitive knowing was still new, and I was learning to trust it fully. I had been working with this client for a while, and while he respected my insights, I knew his trust in me wasn't yet absolute.

The moment he mentioned the new president's name, it hit me like a freight train. My stomach churned violently, and I felt a wave of nausea so intense it nearly dropped me to the ground. It wasn't just a passing feeling—it was a visceral, undeniable knowing.

I looked at him, the words spilling out before I could second-guess myself:

"This man is a sheep in wolves' clothing. With every ounce of me, I'm telling you—run. Don't trust him. He's not what he appears to be. He's manipulative and cruel. Please, be cautious."

My client listened, but I could see the doubt in his eyes. He respected me, but this was a man he had known and trusted for years. To him, my warning seemed impossible, almost absurd.

The Aftermath

Despite his hesitation, my client chose to proceed. Within 11 days of the new president stepping into his role, everything unraveled. The man orchestrated a corporate takeover, leaving my client with absolutely nothing—no position, no paycheck, no connection to the company he had built.

It was devastating to witness. My client was blindsided, left reeling from betrayal. And while I felt a deep sadness for what he endured, I also experienced a profound realization: my insight had been spot on.

That moment changed everything for me. It wasn't just a confirmation of my gift—it was a turning point in how I trusted myself and my intuition. I realized that doubting what I knew to be true served no one—not me, not my clients, and not the work I was here to do.

A Lesson in Awareness

From that experience, I learned to approach my insights with unwavering confidence, but also with compassion for those who weren't ready to see what I saw. I began to frame my intuitive guidance in a way that allowed clients to hold space for the possibility, even if they couldn't fully grasp it in the moment.

I now tell my clients:
"You may not see this right now, and that's okay. Take the information, put it in the back of your mind, and just watch. Be aware. When the time comes, you'll know."

This approach helps clients stay open to the guidance without feeling overwhelmed or resistant. It gives them the freedom to observe and make their own decisions while keeping my insights as a trusted resource.

Trusting the Gift

That experience taught me to never let someone else's doubt overshadow my knowing. My intuition doesn't come from ego or guesswork, it comes from a connection to something far greater.

The lesson was clear: trust what comes through, even when others don't yet understand it. Because when the truth reveals itself, as it always does, the impact of that knowing can be life changing.

This story serves as a powerful reminder of the importance of trusting your gifts, standing firm in your truth, and offering guidance with both confidence and compassion. It's a balance I've carried with me ever since, one that has deepened my work and the relationships I build with my clients.

Going Beyond Logic

The sixth sense is about more than instinct—it's about alignment. It's the bridge between logic and intuition, between what we think we know and the infinite wisdom that exists beyond it. Fully embracing this gift has transformed how I approach every aspect of my life and work.

Each time I channel, I feel the connection to something greater. It's not a guessing game, it's a direct line to clarity, guidance, and purpose. And the more I trust it, the stronger it becomes.

Why the Sixth Sense Matters

Napoleon Hill describes the sixth sense as the highest form of intelligence, the key to unlocking your fullest potential. When you embrace this gift, you align with a flow of energy and wisdom that guides your decisions, accelerates your growth, and connects you to limitless possibilities.

The sixth sense is about trusting yourself, even when logic tells you otherwise. It's about leaning into the unknown with faith that the answers will come, and they will always lead you to your highest good.

Practical Tools for Embracing Your Sixth Sense

1. **Quiet the Mind**

   o   Create space for intuition by practicing stillness and mindfulness. Intuition thrives in calm, focused energy.

2. **Set Intentions**

   o   Before seeking answers, set a clear intention: *What do I need to know? What guidance will serve my highest good?*

3. **Tune Into the Energy**

- Pay attention to the subtle shifts in energy when a thought, idea, or action feels right. Your body often knows before your mind catches up.

4. **Trust the First Feeling**

   - Intuition speaks quickly and clearly. Avoid overanalyzing—your first instinct is often the most accurate.

5. **Practice with Small Decisions**

   - Strengthen your intuitive muscle by using it for everyday choices, building confidence in its guidance over time.

The sixth sense is your greatest ally, a gift that connects you to the limitless wisdom of the Universe. Are you ready to trust it fully?

Create space for your intuition. Lean into the knowing, even when it defies logic. Because when you embrace the power of the sixth sense, you unlock a level of clarity, confidence, and purpose that transforms everything.

The answers you seek are already within you, waiting for you to listen, trust, and act.

Affirmations for Intuitive Alignment

1. *I trust my intuitive knowing and embrace the wisdom it provides.*

2. *I am aligned with infinite intelligence and receive guidance effortlessly.*

3. *My intuition is clear, strong, and always aligned with my highest purpose.*

4. *I release doubt and trust the clarity of my inner voice.*

5. *I am guided by the wisdom of the Universe in every decision I make.*

Chapter 13

Face Your Fears - Conquering the Final Barrier

"Fears are nothing more than a state of mind." –
Napoleon Hill

Fear is the invisible barrier that stands between where we are and where we want to be. Napoleon Hill understood that fear, more than any external obstacle, is what keeps people from achieving their fullest potential. To overcome it, we must first recognize it and then confront it with unwavering determination.

For me, overcoming fear has been a central theme throughout my journey. Fear isn't something that disappears, it's something you learn to move through. Each step forward required me to face fears head-on, whether they were fears of criticism, failure, or the unknown.

Facing Criticism

When I first stepped fully into my role as an intuitive business strategist, I knew I would face criticism. The voices of doubt from others were loud:

"Are you sure this will work? People might think you're crazy!"

Even those closest to me worried that my work would make me vulnerable to judgment, questioning not only my methods but even my mental stability. The fear of criticism loomed large, threatening to paralyze me.

But I couldn't let it. I believed in my vision too deeply. I knew that if I let the fear of what others thought dictate my actions, I would be shrinking into a version of myself that wasn't true to who I was.

I remembered something Eleanor Roosevelt said:

"No one can make you feel inferior without your consent."

So, I made a conscious choice: I would not give anyone the power to diminish me. Instead, I focused on those who understood my work, who resonated with my energy, and who saw the value in what I offered. Slowly, the criticism lost its sting, and I found strength in staying true to myself. I wasn't here to convince anyone. I was here to share with those that are ready.

The Fear of Failure

The fear of failure was another constant companion, especially as I began creating the Center for Creators. The vision was massive, the stakes were high, and there were moments when the weight of it all felt crushing.

What if it didn't work? What if I couldn't pull it all together?

Those fears whispered in the back of my mind, but I refused to let them hold me back. Instead, I reframed failure not as an end but as a step on the path to success. Every time I felt that fear creeping in, I reminded myself: *This isn't about avoiding failure, it's about learning, evolving, and moving forward.*

Letting Go of Control

Perhaps the greatest fear I had to overcome was the fear of uncertainty. As someone who has always loved to plan, stepping into the unknown was terrifying. Leaving a secure yet unaligned situation—whether in business or my personal life—felt like stepping off a cliff without knowing if there was a net.

I vividly remember a moment when I had to choose between staying in a situation that felt safe but stifling or venturing into the unknown, trusting that a better path would unfold. Everything in me wanted to cling to the familiar, but I knew I couldn't grow if I stayed where I was.

So, I let go.

It wasn't easy, and there were moments of doubt, but as I released control, something incredible happened. Opportunities began to appear, solutions unfolded, and I found myself surrounded by the very people and circumstances I had been hoping for—proof that the Universe always meets you when you take bold, aligned action.

Why Overcoming Fear Matters

Fear is a natural part of growth, but it doesn't have to define us. Hill's wisdom reminds us that fear is nothing more than a state of mind, and like any state of mind, it can be changed. By facing our fears, we take back our power and open ourselves to possibilities that fear would otherwise keep hidden.

Each time I faced a fear—whether of criticism, failure, or the unknown—I grew stronger. The fear didn't go away, but my courage grew louder than the fear, and that made all the difference.

Practical Tools for Overcoming Fear

1. **Name Your Fear**

    o   Write down what you're afraid of and why. Bringing it into the light diminishes its power.

2. **Reframe Failure**

    o   Shift your perspective: failure is not the opposite of success but a necessary part of the journey.

3. **Take Small Steps**

   o Conquer fear incrementally. Start with small, manageable actions to build confidence.

4. **Visualize Success**

   o Imagine yourself overcoming the fear and achieving your goal. Feel the relief and pride as if it's already happened.

5. **Lean Into Faith**

   o Trust that the Universe is working in your favor, even if you can't see the full picture yet.

What fear is holding you back? What step are you afraid to take?

Face it. Name it. Move through it.

Because when you choose to confront fear with courage and faith, you unlock a world of possibilities. The barriers that once felt insurmountable begin to dissolve, and you step into a version of yourself that is stronger, wiser, and more aligned than ever before.

The life you want is on the other side of fear. Take the step. Move forward. And trust that the path will rise to meet you.

Affirmations for Overcoming Fear

1. *I release fear and embrace the courage within me.*

2. *I am capable of achieving my goals, regardless of challenges or criticism.*

3. *I trust the process and know that the Universe supports my growth.*

4. *Each step forward strengthens my confidence and clarity.*

5. *Fear does not define me—my actions and resilience do.*

Evolve Beyond Limits

Evolving is not a destination—it's a relentless journey of stepping beyond the known, embracing the discomfort of growth, and discovering the extraordinary within yourself. Each step forward requires courage, faith, and the willingness to venture into the unknown. But the rewards are immeasurable.

When you push yourself out of your comfort zone, you open doors to possibilities you never imagined. You experience the fullness of life, not as a spectator, but as an active participant in your own evolution. It is through these moments—when you feel stretched, uncertain, and even uncomfortable—that you grow into the person you are meant to be.

A Life of Infinite Expansion

Every principle you've explored in this book is a guidepost on the path of infinite expansion. Each one pushes you to align your thoughts, actions, and beliefs with the person you are becoming. Together, they form a blueprint for living a life that is not only meaningful but transcendent.

This journey doesn't end—it evolves every day. The Universe is always conspiring to uplift and inspire you, to surprise and delight you in ways that expand your mind, body, and soul. The work is never finished, and that's the beauty of it.

Explore. Receive. Live in the fullness of your connection to something greater.

Step Into Your Infinite Potential

As you move forward, remember this: evolution is infinite. Each day is an opportunity to rise higher, dream bigger, and grow deeper into the truth of who you are, what your purpose is and the legacy you are here creating.

Allow the Universe to guide you. Allow the unknown to shape you. And trust that every step you take is leading you toward something greater than you could ever imagine.

Infinite expansion continues to unfold, uplifting and inspiring, filling every corner of your being with the joy of becoming. Step boldly into the life you were meant to live. Your potential is limitless, and your time is now.

About the Author

Christie Russ is an intuitive business strategist, Oracle, author and thought leader committed to empowering individuals to unlock their highest potential. A trailblazer in personal evolution and innovation, Christie has guided top executives, entrepreneurs, and high achievers to redefine their lives, businesses, and legacies. Drawing from her own remarkable journey of resilience and reinvention, Christie combines a modern twist to timeless wisdom, cutting-edge technology, and deep intuitive insights to help others overcome obstacles, rise above limitations, and create a life of purpose and abundance. Her revolutionary approach merges the practical with the spiritual, inspiring profound breakthroughs that ripple into lasting, global impact.

As the Founder and CEO of *Center for Creators*, Christie is at the forefront of integrating blockchain technology, AI, live streaming holograms, the Metaverse and personal transformation to shape the future of conscious leadership. Her unwavering dedication to growth and evolution has earned her recognition as a mentor and guide for those ready to lead extraordinary lives.

With her unique ability to illuminate pathways to success and fulfillment, she is not only changing lives but also elevating humanity's collective potential.

ChristieRuss.com

CenterForCreators.com

CFCRewards.com

LinkedIn: @christie-jackmond-russ
Facebook: @christie.j.russ
Instagram: christie_russ_

NOTES

NOTES

NOTES

www.ingramcontent.com/pod-product-compliance
Lightning Source LLC
Chambersburg PA
CBHW060822120626
46557CB00001B/333